COPY NO. 2

KV-419-254

Tuesday – Sunday
T +44 (0)20 79?
F +44 (0)20
poetrylih

Le

WITHDRAWN FROM THE POETRY LIBRARY

BORROWED LIGHT

ESSENTIAL POETS SERIES 121

Canadä

ONTARIO ARTS COUNCIL
CONSEIL DES ARTS DE L'ONTARIO

Guernica Editions Inc. acknowledges the support of
The Canada Council for the Arts.
Guernica Editions Inc. acknowledges the support of
the Ontario Arts Council.
Guernica Editions Inc. acknowledges the Government of Ontario through
the Ontario Media Development Corporation's Ontario Book Initiative.
Guernica Editions Inc. acknowledges the financial support of
the Government of Canada through the Book Publishing Industry
Development Program (BPIDP).

MERLE NUDELMAN

BORROWED LIGHT

POETRY LIBRARY
SOUTHBANK CENTRE
ROYAL FESTIVAL HALL
LONDON SE1 8XX

GUERNICA
TORONTO · BUFFALO · CHICAGO · LANCASTER (U.K.)
2003

Copyright © 2003, by Merle Nudelman and Guernica Editions Inc.
All rights reserved. The use of any part of this publication, reproduced,
transmitted in any form or by any means, electronic, mechanical, photo-
copying, recording or otherwise stored in a retrieval system, without the
prior consent of the publisher is an infringement of the copyright law.

Antonio D'Alfonso, editor
Guernica Editions Inc.
P.O. Box 117, Station P, Toronto (ON), Canada M5S 2S6
2250 Military Road, Tonawanda, N.Y. 14150-6000 U.S.A.

Distributors:
University of Toronto Press Distribution,
5201 Dufferin Street, Toronto, (ON), Canada M3H 5T8

Gazelle Book Services, Falcon House, Queen Square,
Lancaster LA1 1RN U.K.

Independent Publishers Group,
814 N. Franklin Street, Chicago, Il. 60610 U.S.A.

First edition.
Typesetting by Selina.
Printed in Canada.

Legal Deposit – Fourth Quarter
National Library of Canada
Library of Congress Catalog Card Number: 2003101165.

National Library of Canada Cataloguing in Publication
Nudelman, Merle
Borrowed light / Merle Nudelman.
(Essential poets series ; 121)
Poems.
ISBN 1-55071-180-6
1. Jews–Canada–Poetry. 2. Holocaust, Jewish (1939-1945)–Poetry.
I. Title. II. Series.
PS8577.U34B67   2003   C811'.6   C2003-901155-0
PR9199.4.N83B67 2003

Contents

In a Polish Village 9
Kalman's First Friends 10
Grave 11
Wedding Day 13
Pogrom in Kielce 14
Schooling 17
The Journey 18
Lily 20
The Singer 21
Magical Shoes 22
The Polka 23
The Sabbath Queen 24
Boarders 26
Evening Ritual 27
Sleepwalking 28
Playing at Tyranny 29
Mama's Helper 30
Ancestral Shadows 32
Food Warfare 34
Tender in Chocolate..36
Marilyn 38
Hair 39
Walking 40
Comforting 41
The Runner..43
Schindler's List 44
Passover 45
Hands 46
Silence, 1944 47
Teeth 48
The last time I see you...49
Daughter 50
Boxes 51
The Visit 52
Atonement...53
The Worker..54

August Morn 55
Traces 56
Black and White 57
The Home Front 59
Farm Ride 60
Storming 61
Song Bird 62
Faces 64
Holding Hands with Tatte 65
Laughter 66
Hollow Prayers 67
Inhaling 69
Presto 70
The Finding 71
My Movie Star 77
Night Visions 78
Spit and Shine 79
Daddy's Girl 80
The Inheritance 81
Moving 82
Child-Hands..83
Stone 84
Unveiling...85
Grounding 86
Snow falls and I 87
In Silk 88
I step lightly 89
Circle Dance..90

Glossary...91
Acknowledgements 92

For my parents

And God saw the light, that it was good:
and God divided the light from the darkness.

Genesis, Chapter 1

In a Polish Village

Leah, seventeen, composed,
a precious meteor blushing,
is betrothed.
Aaron, scholar, voice lyrical,
ambles into the parlour,
hat in hand,
stoops into armchair creases.
Whisked away, he bumps onto the rug,
wags a finger at bobbing black curls.
She poses for hours in emerald satin,
head tilted at cobwebs, dreaming
as her likeness emerges in vivid oils.
Villagers toast l'chaim, stomp whirling hora
amidst noodle puddings and foot-high tortes.

1939

wedding plans halt
the future vanishes

Kalman's First Friends

We swelled the streets
of our neighbourhood in Kielce,
shouting, joking, cheers tumbling
like a roll on my snare drum.
Handsome guys – girls liked us,
let us sneak a kiss.
Winters, we sailed across the ice,
triangles of wood sharp with metal strips
tied to our shoes.
Summers, we played street-soccer,
kicked a ball of suit scraps begged
from Papa's tailor shop.

We thought those days would grow.
The Nazis cut them into the dirt.

Grave

i
They force-march
female worker-prisoners
in rows of five
along Polish country road.

They stumble, suffer
beatings, cursed commands:

> *Rise*
> *or be killed.*

ii
She trudges, head bent,
merges with the striped mass,
lifts one foot
in front
of the other.

iii
He points with his gun
to the clearing.

She obeys,
thinks
her beauty bears
food.

iv
"Stand there, Jew,
next to the pit
closer, hands at your side
completely still."

He raises his gun,
takes aim at the woman,
prepares to shoot.

v
An officer growls,
"Nein,"
and the guard
lowers his gun.

Wedding Day

Gentle in sepia tones
the solemn couple, heads touching,
rest heavy eyes on the camera's heart.
They look beyond the tiny bridal circle
to shadow faces, phantom witnesses to this hasty day,
short months after the war.
She in a suit of navy, notched collar of white,
unadorned waves loosening at her neck.
He in white shirt, cravat and grey tweed.
Borrowed clothes, borrowed light.
Two lost children grasping.
In the brown cave of their eyes burns
the blackness of knowing.

Pogrom in Kielce

i
To Kielce they return.
They seek slivers
of their lives.

They room
at 7 Planty Street
in a boardinghouse.

ii
July 4, 1946.

Kalman strolls
to the barbershop
at the end of the street,
passes dozens running.

He races to No. 7.

iii
They barricade doors
while police shout,
"Out! Men first!"

They open the door,
file past police
with rifles cocked.

iv

Kalman kisses his bride
goodbye, leaves Leah
wrapped in a robe of pink.

Steps from the street he hears
killing sounds
and darts to the attic
where two men hide.

v

The baker enters her room.

Leah quakes. She squeezes
scant dollars in hands
pocket-burrowed.

He goes.

vi

Two climb higher
near the attic door.
"Come out," they taunt.
"Come out."

vii

Leah leans on Kalman's arm
as they walk down Planty Street,
its cobblestones ruby, floating
in the half-light of dusk.

Schooling

They are students a few short years,
he in Kielce, she in Bodzentyn,
then apprentice in family business
before the Germans come.
Both start other training –
slaving in work camps, begging bread.
Their skin grows calloused to the sting
of blood raining about them.
They stumble out of the barracks
into each other's arms and together scavenge.
Canada calls for tailors and he
passes the test.
They graduate to the New World.

The Journey

i
Carried on the *Samaria*
over the ashen waters
we emigrate to an unknown home,
distant from the Polish village
where I grew and lost
family and dreams.

ii
I yearn for Palestine,
our sun-baked land,
to midwife oranges
from that mother-soil.

iii
In America, he says,
our future awaits
like a blooming tulip
poised to open rosy.

iv
Thoughts of my village-home
recede with the shoreline and
I weep in bitter loneliness.

v
The endless ocean
huge with swelling waves
rocks me seasick,
a girl-woman pregnant
with my first –
a child to be born strong
in the shelter of golden streets.

Lily

Some call her Lily, thinking
Leah sounds Old World.
Their immigrant ears spurn
the breathy softness of an *L*
followed by a sigh.
Lily, brilliantly orange
standing upright on her thick stalk.
She was given the name of Leah,
first wife of a deceived Jacob,
now renamed,
drowning out mother's calls,
sisters' voices singing her home,
sighing at trickster Leah.
Leahla, little Leah lost.

The Singer

Weekend visitors cluster in the kitchen
elbows resting on the round table.
Lined faces press forward debating,
sharing allusions to that other life,
that Polish birthplace.

They turn to Leah,
pliant as a melody.
>   *Sing for us, Leah,*
>   *of that Shtetl Beltz,*
>   *of that Mama dear.*

Ghosts of the shtetl float fragrant
from Leah's lips. She reaches deeper,
tears away musical scraps
until her voice soars,
breaks light, sound into prisms.

They listen, skin goosefleshed,
and their minds move inward
to contented childhood days,
a simple life vanquished
with the final notes of song.

Magical Shoes

She slips into open-toed pumps,
clear plastic with rows of rhinestones
on three inch heels.
When she walks the shoes disappear,
only the twinkles of those stones linger.
They are magical like Cinderella's glass slippers.
She clicks her heels three times
but remains rooted in this Canadian soil.

The Polka

Crystal earrings dangle free
from curls pulled high.
Swirls of chiffon swish on her hips
as silver feet tap in time with the big band.
Couples waltz on mirrored walls, gowns
chiseled jewels under chandelier light.
The ballroom wears a scent
of carnations and roast beef.
She spins on sound with her Gene Kelly
pumping her arms to the polka beat.
Her skin sings electric.

The Sabbath Queen

i
Roasting smells of the Sabbath meal
warm the night, wet our mouths
as we wait dressed in finery.
You crown black waves with creamy lace

then, like a bride, approach the linen cloth,
near the brilliance of the silver candelabra.
You flame the wicks of stocky white candles,
circle silvery branches thrice, beckon

the Sabbath Queen. Eyes finger-veiled,
you drift in a moment golden and eternal
intone the blessing, your prayer
spilling hope.

ii
On the counter, translucent bowls –
cream edged in gold washed peach at dusk.
Mother stirs a pot of chicken soup and I
bounce at her side, eyes level with the burners.

She ladles bountiful servings and into broth
plops triangular kreplach. Plump
with beef and liver, pungent with garlic and onions.
We ease the bowls onto the dining room table

pristine in crocheted lace. Father pours
sacramental wine. Blessings sung, I bend close
to kreplach floating in a soupy haze. My china bowl
rings when silver-touched as I section kreplach

into mouth-size bites, capture a sliver with broth, carrot.
Spoon pressed to lips, I puff cooling breath, inhale
perfume of chicken stock mingled with spiced meat.
Taste. Dough firm, filling rough on my tongue.
The bowl shines empty.

Boarders

A parade of boarders marches
through our fourth bedroom.
Varied, like garden pebbles.
The gaunt Fuller Brush salesman,
the alcoholic shoe clerk,

then the chain-smoking realtor
sits at the breakfast nook,
drops crumbs of his life
onto speckled linoleum.
The smoker shuffles away.

Flamenco dancers from Madrid,
Ramon and Rita, roost.
Hair black as a crow's wing,
skin of olive hue, hands that cut the air.
Rita clicks ebony castanets,

slips their concave smoothness
onto my fingers.
They snap across the television stage –
she in ruffled red, he in sleek black.
Ruby spirals in tangerine light.

Evening Ritual

Twilight – workday closes,
household chores done.
Dinner waits warming,
table set gleaming.
I post fleece slippers at the door,
aligned sentries vigilant
for Dad's kiss-filled return,
and follow you upstairs.
You select a fresh dress,

smooth away imagined creases
with the sure strokes of your hands,
move to the bathroom's mirrored brightness.
With a powdery pink puff
you pat the contours of your heart-shaped face,
then with wetted fingertip trace the curve
of your arched eyebrows. Lips reddened,
you lift your brush,
pull it through hair black, luxuriant

again and again until the waves
shimmer in reflected light.
With hair swept behind seashell ears
you twirl shining locks around your fingers,
form curl-rolls at the side and back,
finish with a soft wave flowing onto your brow.
Content, you turn,
take my hand and together
we descend.

Sleepwalking

She is stranded in treeless mud-streets,
suburban 1950s Toronto.
Torn by husband from mid-town friends
she floats in her split-level prison,

clutches telephone-ties like plasma.
She wears homemaker uniform
              housedress, apron
and dusts, polishes, irons

irons, polishes, dusts
until the house shines
like an apple for hubby's nod.
She sculpts her days

around school bells,
home-from-work hubby,
hours punctuated by breakfast and lunch,
by dinner steaming on green arborite.

She was once a lilac butterfly,
now earthbound, a caterpillar
crawling on her belly in shadows
head averted, eyes blinking.

She shrivels.

Playing at Tyranny

Sitting around the kitchen table
we game away Saturday afternoons.
Monopoly board set, we hunt our rivals,
prowl pastel streets pursuing, being pursued.

We taunt our opponents, trade gibes
with hoarded properties, wear power.
We grow large in our chairs
and play on until one ascends

victor of the bankrupt and shattered.

Mama's Helper

i
We descend steep wooden steps,
brush pitted walls reeking of dankness.
Beneath dusty light the washer hugs twin sinks,

wears a crown of beige wringers.
Snaking hose shoots steam as the hulk grunts,
drags aprons, nighties down into churning waters.

We lift leaden cloth from the heaving tub,
guide it through shifting gums, rinse in clear pools.
In the yard our puckered hands peg the week

to the metal line that sings forward with a nudge.
Sheets, shirts, socks balloon into the blue of day,
flap-snap dry, fold into sunny wicker.

ii
Summer vacation
I iron dishtowels wrinkle-free,
pluck quills from fatty chicken skin,
polish hardwood, scrub dishes,
wait for the sweet "You're wonderful."
I am waiting still.

iii
"A girl makes babies. That's what she's for," Mother sighs.
Her eye-slits slice me open, scrape me
hollow like a green melon.
A girl, just a girl.

Ancestral Shadows

i

A town tucked in verdant farmland
peopled with Poles and Jews.
Circle of shops, school, church
and a synagogue at its heart.
I try to picture grandparents, lost sisters,
ask mother the colour of hair, eyes' shape.
She winces.
"Did Bubie look like her? Were my aunties
pretty? Was Zaidie wise?"
Disembodied names, rivers of lives
rippling to the parted Red Sea.
Writings, photos vanished,
sacred heirlooms scattered.
We clutch charred gossamer.

ii

"You will live a charmed life," she says.
"I have hungered, I have endured
but you, you will grow safe
within the cocoon of my prayer."
Fierce in her mother-bear love, she
trickles honey down my throat
to smooth the day's bitterness,
swipes demons with a growl
from the bowels of her throat,
rings days, nights with her refrain:
Happy. Lucky. Blessed.

iii
My mother never cries.
Her brown eyes are dust-dry,
her throat barred against sobbing.
Then her sister Dora falls into death.
Dora, the eldest, the kind one.
Esther and Fela choke out the news
as she lies awash in fever.
Mother stares with rabid eyes, howls
the dirge of the orphaned wolf
abandoned on a rocky shelf.

Food Warfare

Caught
in the shutter's wink
mother's extended hand
clutching sandwich,
cramming your chipmunk cheeks
as she cajoles,
       "Eat, eat,"
and you no longer a baby
or even little.

Dinner plate weighty
graying mass of potatoes,
meat, limp yellowed beans.
       Grotesque abundance
grabs the throat, chases
tremulous appetite away.

You shake your head,
       "No, no,"
as she prods, begs,
pours guilt over you,
to consume all that – that stuff
       "People starving."

You compress your lips,
swing your hair and snarl,
       "Send it to them."

Mother rethinks her strategy:
> "Eat or else
> I'll call the police,"
and you troop from the kitchen,
retreat to your room, braced at the window
for the police to take you.

They never arrive.

Tender in Chocolate

i

The doorbell rings. He presents a mink coat
tucked in tissue, arranged inside a cardboard box.
Mother parts gauzy sheets, holds the coat to the light,
slips inside fur like velvet chocolate.
Long to the ankles, full and flared in front and back.
A sweep of collar caps shoulders,
dips inches beneath the nape of her neck.
Fingers kiss throat, lift collar to frame her face.
Glamorous like Marilyn Monroe.
She twirls before the hall mirror, revels in the swing.
We race to her side, hug furry curves,
snuggle our faces in warmth. Our hands leave tracks
as we iron the folds up and down, up and down
fingering depths.
She melts into shades of brown.

ii

She cherishes her coat of mink,
strokes its lengths like a lover's loins,
stores it within cedar closet walls
safe from moths and fleas.
Later, she lets the furrier
remodel her mink.
He carves away the rich flares,
the sweeping collar,
creates a coat short and boxy,
leaves the glamour
on the cutting room floor.
She wears that coat unchanged.
When her heart gives out,
I carry that fur home.

Marilyn

Inside the wooden cottage I swat a frenzy
of flies fling-pinging against the screen.
Wings twitch with each thwack of rubber.
Outside, I flop onto a towel of red
levitating on stubbly grass.
Radio news slithers out the door:
Marilyn Monroe found dead.

Crystal droplets explode
onto the fiery ground.

Hair

dark as sable, fine as sand,
with a sheen like rosin
glistening on violin strings.

Hair that hangs in angular lines
framing earlobes in black,
cutting across my brow,

a precise fringe that sways with a nod.
Straight, not like hers,
so lush with curls

that dance as she glides,
capturing light and locking it
within the moon of her face.

Walking

i

We stroll along the sidewalk
under maple branches arched
with leaves of red and green.
Sunlight tweaks my nose.
I tickle your hand enveloping mine,
strain to match your long stride,
the turned-out sureness of your step
as I run-walk down the street.
I tire in the shadow of your footsteps,
mimic your beat, arms swinging at my sides.
You stop. I step onto your feet and you
clasp my hands as we move together,
a father-daughter being
straddling its way to uncle's house.

ii

We march down shaded streets,
my squirmy hand clenched in her fist,
her pace brisk, shoulders squared.
We pass girls jumping a hop-scotch grid,
others bent over marbles, and I glare
at mother intent on errands this summer noon.
I shrink from their pitying looks,
cold eyes appraising my mother –
her tiny stature, voluminous breasts,
old world style of dress and hair.
I hold myself apart, don haughty airs.
I make choices with her as yardstick –
who not to be, how not to look,
how not to live.

Comforting

i
Bedroom walls tremble, daylight pierces,
my skin shines moist.
Drapes of sheerest pink exile the sun.
Your cool fingers weave through my hair,
lips press against my brow.
You bring trays of toast
sweetened with honey,
mugs of meaty broth.
My solicitous handmaiden.
I rejoice in tenderness.

ii
You rest, plump body rigid,
arthritic knees exposed.
My bumbling hands knead clicking joints,
warm your flesh, carve thick circles
until my wrists, fingers throb numb.
You point to humpbacked toes,
soles like tree bark burning
with diabetic heat, and I cluck-cluck,
massage, press, rub,
my spine stiff with ache.
I snatch a glance at the clock,
two minutes more,
then pull free.

iii
I crumple into your young arms,
head cradled in your aproned lap.
You dig your fingers deep
into my thicket of hair,
probe those swells of pain.
I uncurl beneath the compress
of your crooning, surrender
to the chill of cloth binding my brow,
offer up faith in mother-healer
to make me whole.

The Runner

I'm in a race to the finish line.
Days, I charge through school doors on stubby legs,
burst into the bakery for mother's seedless rye,
drag my brother to his kindergarten class.
Nights, I bolt up basement stairs as *The Twilight Zone*
fades to dots, Alfred Hitchcock mumbles goodnight.
Mother asks, "Who's chasing you?"
but I just keep on running
hounded by a boogeyman,
yesterday's not-good-enoughs.
I hunt tomorrow's favour.

Schindler's List

Sliding from the car mother asks,
"What's this film about again?"
She slogs into the theatre's gloom,
drops into her chair, skin pulled close.

Now it unfolds.

"I saw, I was shorn," she says.
Ashes stream.
They inhale their brethren.

Memory racks my mother
fragile survivor
and she shivers.

---

*A movie by Steven Spielberg.

Passover

You drag boxes to the kitchen,
pots and dishes enjoyed one week of the year,
place them scrubbed on lined cupboard shelves
beneath boxes of matzoth, jars of jam.
You scour the house fresh
for eight days of remembering the exodus.
Then, the seder meal – fish for procreation,
carrots with honey for a sweet life.
We recite the story, sing the songs, bite
into bitter herbs dipped in salted water.
Our faces redden from the harshness of horseradish.
Our mouths smart from the cut of tears.

Fifty years after, you speak of your pharaoh,
the lash of the crematorium, links in a barbed chain.

Hands

The hands of a pianist or grand lady
airing a flushed cheek with the flick of her fan.
Now, her fingers are gnarled roots
throbbing with the tremors in her blood.
She shakes her head at the sight of them.

"These hands," she says, "these hands."
"In the camps I carried large rocks knee-deep
into the winter river to dam spring's flow.
I climbed ladders holding strong
the bags of cement."

I stare at her – this woman
who groans at potatoes' weight,
who falls helpless at the lid of a jar.
This stranger, my mother.

Silence, 1944

You tell us little
about the nightmare years,
memories shut away
from daylight's reflection,
bereavement mutely borne.
You leave us strangers
to your gasping moments. Now,
you toss like a snared rabbit
caught in that trauma-trap.
You quiver at the shout of voices,
slump in a corner, hushed
still.

Teeth

She smiles, and even rows
of lightly stained teeth catch your eye.
Teeth like tiny kernels of corn
perfectly matched, clinging to swollen gums.
No ups, no downs, nor pointed canines here.
Surfaces chiselled flat, smooth by years of grinding
fear in the darkness of long nights.
Later, she needs the days as well to crumble her demons
into spit-out dust.

The last time I see you

you wear a maroon dress,
        buttons to the waist,
speak of dreams battering your nights.
       He says,
"She's making me crazy with her worries."

A chastened child, you shake your head,
hobble to the hall for your coat
       of beige wool, whisper,
"He never has a good word for me."
       You take his arm at the door

but he shakes you off –
       pesty fly
and you fumble for walls
       to guide you
down the stairs.

I see the back
of your bent head,
       the stoop of shoulders
as you limp along the path.
       I am waving a smile.

POETRY LIBRARY

Daughter

i

As a child I thought
if you die, I will shrivel
like curls of rose petals.
Your presence primal
like water, like air.
But I live and you
stumble no more
along scarred pathways.
Photos blink incomplete.
Your chair rests barren.
It beckons.

ii

I am an earthenware vessel
shaped in the face of my mother.
I tip and tears slip to the ground.
Water at my feet?
So remote from this pool
lying within, stagnant,
scummed
from years of holding.

Boxes

We go about our lives in beige boxes,
opaque glass with a door at the front.
We carry our boxes with us,
make say-nothing conversation.
Mother dies.
Family files by pressed to their doors,
heads bobbing.
Their walls bump mine.
My boundaries of beige shatter and I bow
for hands to bless my skin
but boxes are shut tight.
I stand alone on those jagged slivers.

The Visit

i

I reach out, dear Mother,
stroke your hand, caress your cheek.
You are regal in an armchair of claret velvet.
I marvel at your lustrous face,
ponder what to ask, to say,
hesitate and you slip away –
a wisp rising in morning mist.

ii

The anniversary of your death falls
on the seventh night of dreams.

I creep through barren corridors,
government green,
pull open the final door,
squint inside.

The chamber is deep. Rows of elders
in blue cotton
recline on starched metal beds.
Propped on pillows, you chat.
These hospital walls, loathsome in life.
"Come home, Mama."
You hug the blanket.

Atonement

Mother, I flinch at the changes in you,
cling to father's tender lies.

My grief is huge at your sudden death,
remorse inflated like a monstrous balloon
crushing me boneless into the earth.

The lumbering child wishing for more.

I lacerate my mind chasing your life,
drag words onto pages wrung dry.

A supplicant, I beg, "Forgive."

The Worker

He tailors away his twenties in Toronto's garment district,
pushing English off his tongue with a Polish-Yiddish twist.
Mornings, he rides the College trolley to Spadina,
arm around the bag of collars he stitched by lamplight.
Piecework.
He remembers his father's careful hands in their shop
in Kielce and works his fingers with speed, skill.
Set-in sleeves sewn without a ripple, fancy trim applied
with artist's care – stitches small and arrow-straight.
Boss-man pats him on the back, this boyish Ray Milland
with the rakish look, the eager smile.
"Keep up the good work, Kelly."
And so he does – four back-bending, eye-squinting years.
Fed up with waiting for a boost to foreman,
with sweating under the big man's glare,
he tallies his savings,
takes a partner and starts over again.

August Morn

Early light suns the lawn with its edging
of roses and scarlet geraniums.
I skip-hop circles humming,
squint at the sky, recall whispers
snared behind the hall railing.
Sisters, father, mother pushed
into a cattlecar one steamy Polish morn
August, years ago.
Tatte stares into the walls, cheeks
seared with tears.
Innocence, the fraudulent magician,
steals away.

Traces

He looks over his shoulder.
I suck in girlish breath, grab my chance –
       bend close to his left forearm,
       peek at the tender pale flesh.
Broken blue spiders creep up his arm towards the crook
of his elbow. He catches me staring.
"What's that, Daddy?"
He arranges his mouth in a tiny smile, says,
"It's my old telephone number. I put it there, never to forget."
Mama wears her numbers under cover of sleeves,
hastily hidden
when my eyes cloud with query.
I want to run my fingers over the secret
sealed on my parents' skin,
take away the sting that marks them.

Black and White

i

Hockey Night in Canada shoots and scores
across the black and white screen while
Saturday Night at the Movies beckons

from the other channel.
I scream for the Leafs from my carpet sprawl,
join the family chorus.

Johnny Bower wrestles the puck from the air,
Mahovlich flies down the ice.
The glory years.

They snatch the Cup from Montreal foes
and we whoop-yell for our boys.
We know them all.

ii

Father knows best the television drones.
Mrs. Cleaver orbits the father-sun. His wisdom
impeccable, Solomon-like. And she?

She's perfectly groomed in waist-cinched frock,
a string of pearls ringing her throat. She bustles
about pastel rooms plumping up the pillows.

Ralph shakes a beefy fist at his aproned wife, says,
"To the moon, Alice, right to the moon!"
Hand sharp on her hip, she cocks a sour face

at his scowl, slams through the bedroom door
and he twitch-tosses his head.

The Home Front

They throw words like grenades
at their spouse-targets.
They stab the innocent air, jab
at bedded betrayals.
The kitchen swells with
her soprano screeches of
       low class lout,
his tenor bellows of
       spoiled brat.
Screams escalate, send us
scurrying to our rooms.
I press my head under the pillow,
bones rustling at the crack of sound,
pray for peace between these love-haters
unsettled in the minefield of our home.

Farm Ride

We squeeze into our '57 Chevy,
robin's egg blue, waddling to Newark.
Slotted between gift boxes
that shimmy along white vinyl –
me, a dark ribbon wound around the door,
Al, a spring pinging from sweaty seat
to floor hump asking, "We lost?"
Clouds unzip like upended streams.
We wade through country roads
that suck on tires, freckle chrome wings.
Silver Egg Farm shines in our beams.
We turn down the roadway, bump
towards the terraced farmhouse glow.

Storming

Maples in spring toss leafy manes,
scatter sparrows, red-puffed robins.
They sport luxuriant heads in summer,

stretch their arms to wrestle brothers
posted on parallel lawns. We hide-and-seek
under showers of leaves, tumble and turn

on crackly maple flames, speckle
their gray-brown trunks with snow-volleys.

Hurricane Hazel rips down the road,
scatters severed maple limbs.

Bandaged, torn,
they survive.

Song Bird

i
I tiptoe past sleeping parents,
slip outside clutching shoebox,
lid dotted with holes.
Running through the grass
I search for bright plumage,
listen for chirps, spy

three sparrows hopping.
Movements measured
I stalk my quarry.

Two take to the air,
call to their brother
careless of my stealth.

Box open, lid held tight,
I pounce.
My prey flies low,

lands lightly ahead of my fumbling.
We dance zigzag across the lawn,
stop when the sparrow soars.

I shuffle into the silent house longing
for a bird trilling on a swing
like Mrs. Spring's yellow canary.

ii
Skipping to school I hum
melodies of my making,
notes sewn into quilts of lace.

I am sated with these songs
echoing for my ears only
and I clasp this secret,
a talisman I hold safe.

Faces

i

Mother examines my face at angles,
her head cocked to the right, says,
"You're the image of my sister Rivkah."
Then she turns, picks up the dishtowel.
Her neighbour from the Old Country
studies me hard, says, "Just like your Sarah."
Mother nods, father grumbles,
"Impossible. She's like a twin to my Golda."
And so it goes over the years,
the shadows of my aunts playing
across my changing face.

ii

Jill and I on the cool of the back porch
study the summer sky.
Clouds like woolly sheep.
They are country hills, herons' wings.
I look for Bubies' frowning concern,
the rustle of my aunts' love.
"I'm here. Show me your faces."
Jill, snug in the arms of her elders,
wrinkles her nose
at my wind-borne plea.

Holding Hands with Tatte

My left in the mitt of his right
burrows deep like a rabbit
sheltering from the cut
of silvered day.
From girl-child to woman
he seeks my tender fingers
to cradle in his palm.
He taps his thigh, opens his hand
in a ritual of invitation.
He twines his strong-man digits
about my hand,
squeezes sinews with his circling thumb,
mashes thin bones with the bigness
of his love.

Laughter

He sprinkles us with jester words and
wicked light fox trots across his face,
fans the corners of his impish eyes,
strokes his mouth into a *Gotcha* smirk.
We flutter and his grin grows.
A chuckle twirls in his throat,
rolls over and over into a laugh that
drops into his belly, brushes his sides.
He laughs so hard, so true,
his eyes melt and our lips
spring free.

Hollow Prayers

i
A rabbi fashioned of Murano glass
draped in a prayer shawl, cream
with a band of black, a fringe
of clear droplets festooning bony knees.
He clasps a torah scroll to his heart.
She is translucent. Azure with splashes
of white. Light shimmers within her.
Rabbi's beard, toes curl heavenward,
soft grey springs primed to dance
          with torah held high.
An offering, a promise.

ii
Every Saturday he goes to synagogue.
He arrives early, takes his usual seat,
passes the morning chanting psalms,
making small talk with the regulars.
Halfway through he and his brother
retire to the basement for a l'chaim
with the schnapps and herring club.

Now and then, when the rabbi's sermon
preaches divine goodness and love,
Dad shakes his head, face bitter.
"So where was He in Auschwitz?"
Silence hangs from the sanctuary dome
like tears blackened with ash.

iii

He fancies himself a choirboy again,
tall on the beema of that vast temple
in Kielce,
the kiss of his parents' eyes on his brow.
Yiddish songs, sabbath hymns
explode from his chest.
He thirsts for sweet voices
like hers.
His dulcet soprano,
his broken canary.

Inhaling

He breathes like a sparrow after she dies,
sips delicately of air.
Breezes ripple in his chest and he
sighs loneliness into his bent throat.
"Open your ribs like fingers," I say.
He obeys, my father-child, lost
in a forest of ghosts –
parents, sisters and now, wife
calling his name.

Presto

He is my Houdini, my Gable all in one.
Storyteller of daredevil charm,
he guides us through the good-time years,
the peril and fate years of the War.

At nineteen, he pummels work camp iron,
swings a sledge hammer like a metal cape.
Guards gone, he turns to his brother, says,
"Lie down, Hershel. Rest."
A granite wall of family love.

He walks away from that train,
that bullet for stealing bread,
that clubbing massacre in Kielce.

Mama laughs and he lifts
me and Allen, both of us together,
high enough to touch the ceiling.
Our man of steel through all the days.

Mama dies and he transforms.
Stooped elder, arms slender,
shoulders rounded in defeat.
In a flash, he's gone.

The Finding

i
The policeman squints through the gauzy windowpane,
says, "There, on the floor. His legs."
He shatters the silence with his nightstick, reaches
into the tidiness of the house, pries open the door.
They enter, he first – uncle, aunt trailing,
then goes forward alone, bends,
lays his hand on stillness.
He guides them, docile, into the kitchen,
tenders water, words of waiting.
The blackness unfurls, enfolds.

ii
The cottage phone rings. A stranger's voice.
"Stay calm," he says. "Bad news."
I blink dry-eyed, fall from my skin
into the hollow of a woman
that wears my face, my shape.
She stumbles to the door, pours into the car,
crawls home through the gloom of a July night.

iii
There is an aesthetic to symmetry,
a lightness to balance,
but where's the beauty when her trauma
flames in him short years later, to the day?
Silent offerings to the heart's misstep
in the flowering moment of summer.

iv

My midnight eyes, ringed in red, watch
his house ablaze with yellow lights,
the front door gaping wide.
Uncle, aunt huddle in shadows.
The doorway darkens – my brother's silhouette,
no one else.

"I want to see Dad."

But I am moments late and he, hours dead,
delivered to funeral home arms.

v

    We push against air,
stumble into the grey light of the waiting room.
Brick wall, fireplace, deep sofa and chairs
of mute leather,
an open staircase falling down
to the panelled offices,
the morgue.

    A shelf of broken dolls
we sit, attend to the hum
of the director sliding down his list
questions asked, answered
monies paid after we stroll
around the casket room pointing
to oak, to traditional white shroud.

    We caress navy velvet,
the pouch holding his prayer shawl –

fringes I braided with childhood fingers –
and drop our molten eyes as we leave
his mantle in the director's care.

vi
We arc around the director,
heads bowed, eyes streaming,
and he pins a black ribbon
over our hearts.
He intones a brief prayer,
tells us, "Tear the fabric."
We are ripped asunder.

I wear that mourning-badge
seven days,
then bury it
within my darkness.

vii
David piles his bags into the car,
slips on mellow jazz,
pulls out of the Chicago morning
north to Toronto.
His mind sifts memories
back, forth like sand
through an hourglass.

That evening he says
he wants to speak
at his Zaidie's funeral.

He steps to the podium in sailor-navy
exhales crystal bubbles –
his Zaidie's taste for herring and cheesecake,
their mania for the Leafs.
He holds out his voice
clear, steady and we float
in his reverie.

viii
Seven days I crouch,
rise early, rush to prayers,
press bread to my lips.
The days are stones, heavy, the same.
I pour water down my throat,
water to fill emptiness.
Low on the naked sofa frame,
cushions stacked to the side,
I cling to coiled tissues.

Visitors come, and come,
touch my hand, my cheek
say, "Such a shock,"
and move to a chair,
to the table of cakes,
the counter of sticky schnapps.
They nod, tongues thickened.
Father, the shadow dancing
through my rooms.

ix

His legion of friends stumble before me.
Their lips tremble as they murmur
about his cheering calls, his errand-boy ways.
Kalman – everyone's *gut Freund.*
Bruised, their love for him
salves my skin.

x

Lisa takes my hand, says,
"I'd like to move in for the shiva."
She cradles my pieces in her arms,
her black hair a prayer on my cheek.
In the morning kitchen she sets out
plates, soft drinks, cakes
and fresh in afternoon light
returns to warm dinner, ready the table.
At night, callers leave and she sits
at my side, reads my eyes,
shepherds me as I tumble
into my sorrow.

xi
I listen to the fluttering of the walls.
The house breathes.
The doors quiet.
My granite heart bears down
on sodden lungs,
throat knotted like a hangman's noose.
I hear the hiss of my serpentine mind
and know
I am alone.

My Movie Star

Tell me, Father, my golden one,
you have not left me –
me, the pagan who worships
your De Niro looks,
your grip so strong
fingers ache from the squeeze
of your hand.
Were you startled like an oak
snapped by the kiss
of a woodsman's ax?
My words hang
like summer leaves.

Night Visions

Tatte sleeps within the ground.
On the third night I see him walking
uphill in a white cotton shirt, black
skullcap peaked on thinned, silver hair.
At his side, a bike he steers, hands
firm on the handlebars as he climbs
higher, never turning.

Ten days later, he sports ebony hair,
the muscled arms of his forties.
I lie on brocade pillows in a claret room,
tall windows draped in wine velvet.
A newborn sleeps beneath muted light.
"Would you like to hold the baby?"
Just his eye-laughter, no more.

Six weeks pass and I see him in bed.
Prone at his side, I kiss his hand,
stroke his old man cheek.
The life-breath dissolves.
Then, the hearse.
Tatte – first word catches
like a pebble in my throat.

Spit and Shine

He prided himself on being neat –
a sharp part in his brilcreamed hair,
mirrored shoes, shirt and pants on the dressy side.
His suits lined up like soldiers. No clutter
anywhere.

As a boy he buffed his shoes with pocketed cloth,
banished spots from lapels and sleeves
with a little spit, the scrape of his nail.
In work camps he was drilled in Aryan order,
so superior to the sloth of the Poles.

Like a sergeant he patrols our rooms,
his keen eye roaming,
still searching for that dusty vase.

Daddy's Girl

"Daddy, come quickly!"
The child's voice rings across the lake,
swamps my rocking in the hammock.
I rest my book on the lawn and recall
father – crooning me to sleep, defanging
demons with his *Zeit dir nichts geschehen.*
Father, dazzling electricity,
larger than any room can contain.

The Inheritance

He stashes away pennies end to end,
stuffs bills in closet pockets,
ready just in case.
Chestnuts for later,
nuggets for the kids.
He bends her and she stretches
her stipend for food and such,
nods when he shuns travel
and restaurant fare.
She dies and he says,
"I've seen so little,"
talks of trips to Vegas,
a new model car.
Gets as far as *I should* when
blackness takes him.
          They trickle down.
These dollars stained
with fear's sweat,
edges rubbed thin
with time and waiting.

Moving

We sell their house in a blink, sift through
fifty years scented with festive meals, her Chanel.
Here, his satchel branded with *Samaria*'s name,

their Bavarian china trimmed black and gold,
fluted crystal borne from black market days.
We stroke their life-remains divided in rooms –

mahogony tables on curved spindly legs,
avocado dinette set black-edged & stippled.
There, beneath those papers, a brown billfold.

It falls open, oozes DP certificate, hills
of skeletal bodies, scarecrows in stripes,
fingers wound around metal twine.

Child-Hands

Close the door softly
> when you linger in that bedchamber's yellow light,
blankets folded open to vine-shaded sheets.

Close the door softly
> before you go into the summer garden sharp
with pine, with blood red roses.

Close the door softly
> as you leave us, parting kiss and front porch chatter
tender as peaches poached in wine.

Close the door softly
> as you travel through the echo of your vacant rooms,
SOLD impaled on the August-browning lawn.

Close the door softly
> when you slip slowly into that steamy cattlecar,
sisters' child-hands straining to touch.

Stone

I go with my brother to the shop on Bathurst Street.
Granite grave markers squat before dove-grey walls.
Some are black, some silver, others taupe or smoky

with flecks of sunset.
Light grey slabs with surfaces unpolished chill
like poured cement. Black ones are mirrored

like ebony keys – smooth on five sides,
sleek as his pomaded hair.
At the head of the stone, a Star of David

or eternal flame, vine leaves, a string of flowers.
Then words crafted in script ancient, modern
or medieval-bent, letters carved one by one.

We recall her rose-dappled stone, worry-talk
about choices – black or shades of coal.
Side by side at the table, we hunch over text.

His name in Hebrew hovers above a prayer.
Finally, that phrase to spark knowing
who he was, what he was rises from our throats.

Unveiling

A field of scarlet, wind-twisting,
shades my eyes with crimson.
Blood's sweet smell.

We chant prayers, rend
gravestone's cover, reveal
your name granite-etched,

love-talk your life. Liquid
rubies fill my chest, slip
from my tongue. I sway

like a rabbi lost in prayer's
spell, yearn to lay on that
May-morning lawn, palms

pressed to mounded earth,
those rubies glistening
on swells of green.

Grounding

I sink like stone
through rug's grey wool,
the bulk of timber beams,

dropping
down, to grainy cement,
the foundation floor

and further,
to autumn's cooling earth,
lower, through layers

of rock, of clay
deeper
to where it's warm again,

closer
to where you lie

and my longing grows

Snow falls and I

wait in line at Canadian Tire,
snow tires wrapped in white plastic
stuffed into the trunk of my salty car.
I settle into a seat of spotted black,
contemplate machines selling drinks,
sweet and savory snacks.
Bleached patrons shuffle feet,
shift hips as they read scattered
sections of yesterday's news,
those red and green flyers.

In sweeps the blond.
Cosmo-cool with plum lips.
She sashays to a corner chair, trills
into the throat of her lacquered phone,
arcs limbs as she conducts her symphony

of chatter. Then, the man
from Eastern Europe, pre-war vintage,
cap angled, white hair neatly combed.
He carries himself like a valuable package.
I try hard not to think of you,

not to let that heaviness find me again.
A row of empty seats and he chooses one
next to mine, spattering yarns.
I see your tailor-hands cut
a child's trim coat.

In Silk

i

She shimmies into a tube of peach silk
fluted at the breast, Empire style.
It sweeps to ankle's curving.
A ruffle of milky chiffon bordered
in lace of pink and baby blue
arcs across her heart.
This is her bed gown when visitors
crowd the hospital room chiming
mazel tov.

ii

I slip inside this rosy cloth,
see her grown young again –
breasts leaking, gait ripe.
I remember her scent
of summer lilacs, the lilt
of her lullaby as she cradles me,
head pillowed on the flutter
of her breathing.

I step lightly

on autumn streets,
bend beneath the boughs' soft casting off.
I swell, a bellows
engorged with the musk of maples.
Walkways awash in canary yellow,
cardinal red, a tan of fawns.
Waves of leaves – some supple, brittle,
others in pieces lie,
and I?
I am carried to childhood streets
on these currents of earth-perfume.
The sun toasts cloth, a chorus rustles
beneath my feet
and you
tall and strong at my side.

Circle Dance

I cha cha to Vegas,
decked out in diva black,
your locket swinging
beneath my throat.
Ebony lilies, swirls of lace
etched on a gilded sphere.
This, his nuptial offering,
your treasure
strokes laughter, slides
at the spine's shifting.
Within the locket walls
you and he, golden.

Glossary

All words and expressions are in Yiddish unless otherwise indicated. Words of Hebrew origin that have been incorporated into Yiddish are not indicated separately.

Beema: Altar.
Befreiung: (German/ Yiddish) Liberation.
Bodzentyn: Village in Poland.
Bubie: Grandmother.
Gut Freund: (German/Yiddish) Good friend.
Kielce: A city in Poland.
Kreplach: Similar to ravioli.
L'Chaim: To life.
Matzoth: Unleavened bread.
Mazel tov: Literally, good luck; congratulations.
Nein: (German) No.
Rosh Hashanah: Jewish New Year.
Shiva: Week of mourning for the death of a family member.
Shtetl: Jewish village.
Samaria: Name of an ocean vessel.
Tatte: Father.
Zaidie: Grandfather.
Zeit dir nichts geschehen: Nothing will happen to you.

Acknowledgements

I thank the editors of the following publications in which some of the poems in this collection originally appeared, sometimes in different versions: *Parchment*, *Surface & Symbol*, *Canadian Jewish News Literary Supplement*, *Kaleidoscope: An International Journal of Poetry*, and *Pagitica*. "Food Warfare" was awarded an Honorable Mention in the Scarborough Arts Council Poetry Contest 2000. Thanks as well to Laura Lush for her guidance and encouragement; to Ruth Panofsky for her support; to Antonio D'Alfonso for his astute editorial direction; and to my husband Harold for his strength and love.

Merle Nudelman is a lawyer and lives in Toronto. Her poems have appeared in a number of Canadian literary journals. *Borrowed Light* is her first book of poetry.

Printed in
November 2003
at Gauvin Press Ltd., Hull, Québec